THE INDEPENDENT ARTIST
A GUIDE TO THE MUSIC INDUSTRY

By Lee Jones

2018 © Lee Jones

2018 copyright Saturn Publishing. All rights reserved.
Published by Saturn Publishing.

TABLE OF CONTENTS

Introduction
6
    A BRIEF HISTORY OF THE MUSIC INDUSTRY
7
TRADITIONAL RECORD LABEL ERA
8
360 DEAL ERA
10
LABEL SERVICES ERA
11
THE BUSINESS MINDSET
13
BRANDING
16
FUNDING
19
MARKETING
21
INTELLECTUAL PROPERTY
23
COPYRIGHT
24
TRADEMARKS
24
BUILDING A TEAM
25
PUBLISHING
29
NEIGHBORING RIGHTS
30

LICENSING
31

MECHANDISING
33

SHOWS AND TOURS
35

CONTRACTS
37

AFTERWORD
40

About The Author
41

Introduction

This book is for those looking to get into the music industry as an independent music artist, or independent label. Either to further your career, making living as an artist or grow your fan base. As an independent artist myself and the owner or an independent record label, I will highlight personal examples throughout this book.

This book will updated continuously with new editions and information.

I often get interns who just graduated a university or college with a masters, or bachelors in so called "Music Business," but have no clue even the basics of how it all works. This is to pass on them as well as the common musician and someone looking to get started in the business with their own label or related venture.

My history started as a musician. O-Town Records came about in 2013. It was a curiosity at that point but quickly grew into something bigger.

We weren't making any money at the point but having everyone there drew attention to us. We built some amazing contacts out there to some of the biggest names in the biz.

A BRIEF HISTORY OF THE MUSIC INDUSTRY

Over the decades the music industry has gone through stages. Or more known as the record business. Record labels and their artist made the majority of their income from sales of records up until about the late 90s. First came vinyl, cassette tapes, then CD's. Record labels signed artist on traditional recording contracts. The artist only signed on their sales of records. The label gave an advance of a sum of money, partial broken down to be used for recording studio cost, manufacturing etc. The rest of the advance to be used for personal living expenses.

TRADITIONAL RECORD LABEL ERA

The label owned full copyrights, also called (The masters) and would sign on for a number of albums and a time frame. Once the artist released their album, the label was expected to recoup the initial advance. Anything made above that initial investment would go back to the artist, but only a percentage of it. Others working on behalf of the artist would take a percentage of that income as well. The artist manager, the label, and any other individuals who got into a contract with the artist prior to the release.

You see the record label at this point is essentially a bank. An artist needs a loan to live off of while they write and record their music, take care of recording expenses, marketing and so on. A real bank would deem the loan as too risky.

In the minds of artist and the general public, the idea of signing with a record label was the pinnacle of one's career. They have made it. All of the household name artist your hear have gone this route. In those days you could send a demo tape of about your best three songs to the A & R department of a record label. Or you could be discovered by an A & R and be signed to a recording contract.

Many of those big artist did get signed to a recording contract this way. Eventually the demo's got to be too many and labels stopped accepting unsolicited demos.
Many record labels did start out small and independent. But those mainly founded prior to the 1970's grew to become one of the Major Labels. Atlantic, Warner bro's, Capitol, Columbia, EMI etc. Eventually over the years the labels merged and bought out smaller labels to become Label groups. It started out as 6 major groups then consolidated over the years to become 3 major groups that we have today. These became known as the "Majors," controlling a large segment of the music sales, radio play and promotion.

An label founded outside to the Majors became known as Independent. Many Independent labels did spring up during the 80's throughout today without being bought out or joining the Major groups. Many household name artist did start out on Independent labels, then graduate to a Major label for more exposure.

Beginning in the late 90's as the internet began to mature, record sales began to dip. The reason was some sites like Napster allowing P2P peer to peer sharing sites that allowed one individual to upload a mp3 song file, and share it with everyone else on the internet. This took a hit on the music industry because now anyone could get a music for free. I remember collecting CD's and tapes around the late 90's early 2000's and making mixes. But being introduced to sites and applications that would torrent music for free. Around the same time the iPod was introduced and Mp3 players took off.

The iPod was the premier mp3 player but there were others as well for those who couldn't afford the expensive iPod. Probably the last time I used a portable CD player was back 2004. Then people were using the mp3 players. So I would go to the computer and rip CD's from windows media player and now the music on the computer.

Then I could transfer those mp3 song files to my mp3 player and any other sources download from Napster for example.

The days of carrying around one CD in your portable CD was over. You now had access to hundreds and even thousands of songs.

Ringtones sales around the early 2000's took off for a while it was a big deal. But overall record sales continued to slump.

360 DEAL ERA

Then came the introduction of the Artist and Record Company Multiple rights agreement deal. Also wildly know as the 360 deal. Records were not selling anymore and labels needed a new revenue stream. With the 360 deal they looked to take a percentage of revenue from everything the artist was doing. From tours, to publishing royalties, to endorsements and sponsorships.

You see the record business is not stable. On any record label rosters you will have the mega stars, the household names. Then you will have the lesser known artist. The majority of lesser known artist do not do so well. They may not even pay back their advance and the label ends up dropping them and ending the contract. The mega stars are expected to not only bring the majority of revenue to the label, but also make up for the failed artist that we're dropped.

The 360 deal kept the record business afloat. But many of those big artist, after their contract was up decided to go independent. They had their name, their brand well known and now they could retain their rights and full revenue.

Artist were now being scouted differently in this 360 era. Instead of finding the unknown singing in an open mic night or sending in a demo, you had to already prove yourself by yourself. It was almost to the point that you really didn't need a label to help boost your career because you did it yourself. You grew your fanbase, made sales and did it all yourself.

Up incoming artist and bands were being scouted online from websites like Myspace and Youtube. They were doing so well generating views, new fans and revenue that the labels wanted a cut. Artist still did sign on because the labels did still have a foothold on the industry, terrestrial radio play, worldwide distribution, major exposure contacts.

LABEL SERVICES ERA

Enter the Label Services era. The traditional record deal has almost vanished. 360 deals are now common among the majors. But as the late 2000's entered into the early 2010's, more artist are independent. There are more avenues now for independent artist to release their music. Major platforms like iTunes have opened their store to independent distributers. Indie distributer include for example CD Baby, Tune core, and more.

By 2015 the music industry model has changed. The majority of Artist no longer sign with record labels at all. But they still need the support of a label. You see it is so easy and accessible now to release your music to the world, and become a recording artist on your own but that now presents new problems. The internet is now flooded with music, the good, the bad and the ugly.

You have from one spectrum the really talented amazing musicians to the really bad. If everyone is releasing their music how do you stand out? How do you get heard? Enter label services. The artist is independent but hires the label for their services. Say I want to tap into the worldwide distribution that the label offers. I can sign an agreement only for the distribution. The label doesn't touch anything else.

So I need help with marketing. The label has the knowledge and know how to get marketing for your music and image to the right avenues. They're an expert in this. Experts from booking shows, marketing, publishing, recording, etc. The independent artist CANNOT do everything. They cannot expect to succeed on their own. You need a team to push you forward. The label services helps with that because you have the support of the label without the label retaining your copyrights, trademarks and revenue.

You can only get so far on your own. Now as we are in the new era of the music industry, the Majors are signing not based on talent or singing ability, but raw numbers. Such individual might not be even a musician or singer but has many followers on social media. They are offered a multi million dollar record deal.

THE BUSINESS MINDSET

The artist must at first get into the right mindset. He/she must realize that you are not only an artist but a booking agent, graphic designer, publisher, lawyer, and so much more. When you are first starting out you might be the most amazing singer, guitarist etc. But that does not really matter right now. No one cares to discover you, you cannot simply record a demo and send that to an A & R. It is not enough to simply be an artist at this point. You must realize that you are a small business at this point.

You can be the must amazing technically talented guitarist the world has never heard of but only play in your bedroom. Why? Because that guitarist has no business sense. Your only good at one thing which makes you useless in this new model of the music industry. You cannot just be amazing at guitar. You must know how to market, make deals, make and sell your product, distribution and more.

You see this early DIY approach is what taught me business. It's what got me interested in business in general. It teaches you the right characteristics such as discipline, persistence, leadership, decision making and so much more.

Why is the employee of a restaurant paid so little but the restaurant generates a million a year in revenue? Because the employee only knows one thing, and can only do one thing. They can make a good burger, but if you cannot market it, sell it and fulfill the orders effectively the business will go belly up. Without executing all the other aspects it will not work at all.

So, stop trying to learn 1000 chords on the guitar(an example) and start thinking how you are going to market yourself and your music, the way this industry works is not the most talented to make it to the top. But those who were able to effectively market and sell themselves growing their fan base offering something of value.

You are wondering how am I able to be a graphic designer, photographer, web developer, booking agent and so and so on. That's one of the benefits of the business mindset. If you are taking the DIY approach you learn. You learn by doing it. You are learning many skills and building your character at the beginning. Yes I said label services is great but that is later on. You learn a bit of these things, you might not become an expert at each but you will be pushed along farther if didn't know jack shit. It's your only choice at this point for most people because they don't have the cash to fund services. We will cover that more in the next chapter.

Once you grow your brand, you can now take on label services to handle your growth.

BRANDING

Just like I stated in the previous chapter your a small business and with every business comes a brand. Think of yourself that way, your not selling scrubbing pads, phone cases, or watches the product is YOU. You see overall you need a professional image.

Artist will usually have something called a press kit. But in this digital era it is called an EPK or electronic press kit. It includes high quality professional quality photos, a well written bio (brief and long version), and files to songs or videos compressed in a zip folder. The brief version of the bio will usually highlight a span of the artist career. No one cares that you went to school and you played a certain instrument. We need to know highlights of your career, accomplishments such as awards or playing a sold out show. It was also include a line or 2 from press reviews in the brief bio. If you don't have the big accomplishments such as selling an arena, include the smaller accomplishments.

The long version of the bio is the same as the brief but includes more details. Add more bulk to it and even can include the mundane details.

Your photos must be taken by a professional photographer. You need to do a photo shoot. It will be used for album covers, press, flyers, social media and your website. Do a photo shoot at least once a year to keep it updated. Do a few headshots, full body shots and sitting shots in at least 2 different outfits. If you play an instrument do some shots with and without it. Don't do the band shots on the railroad tracks, it's been done too many times be creative!

You need a website. It is very important. Include your music, videos, photos, bio, upcoming shows, social media links and contact page. Always refer potential business contacts to your website first. Also invest in a custom domain name. Don't go and get a WIX page with a WIX domain name and call it a day. You need your custom domain name with a dot com. There are many platforms for just dragging and dropping a website to build it you don't need to be a web developer to get a website made.

Social media comes second. Get your custom social media links setup.

Do the graphic design work to create the banners for your page. Don't just upload a photo and think it will look good or fit. It does need to be custom created. Update the banner or profile pic regularly to include text or photos promoting for example and upcoming show or release. It may not be the best right now but it's professional thats going to help further along.

Make sure you are getting all friends to follow your social media profiles so you can start building your numbers.

FUNDING

You probably wondering I need to be a graphic designer, a web developer, a photographer and so on and so on. At first you need to learn some other skills. With the DIY approach you can you do a lot of things on your own. There is an initial investment of getting your website up and running. If don't have a DSLR or pro quality camera you may need to hire a photographer.

Early financing will have to come out of your pocket.

MARKETING

Many artist are now choosing to offer their music completely free. It's a great marketing tactic. Think of your music and your music videos as marketing tools. You won't make money directly from it but being that it removes a barrier and exposes your product to more people.

But not only offer a bad product for free, offer a really good product for free. Your music still has to be top notch.

Terrestrial radio, also know as FM/AM radio is almost dead at this point. Yes people have radios in the car more increasingly radios are being removed from cars altogether. It's all streaming now or they might have an mp3 playing from the phone. Early on we had a contact with COX media for their radio network but never utilized it. I cannot remember the last time listening to radio.

Technically they cannot take payments from a label (payola) or anyone to play music on their networks. It's supposed to be up to the Deejay or program manager to decide what gets played but radio has changed so much since then. For large radio networks like iHeart Radio(AKA Clear Channel), the playlist is already preprogrammed from their headquarters and gets played from a computer. No one is there actively deejaying the content and less will you hear an announcer.

I would avoid terrestrial radio. It is not worth the effort to invest in a locked down, and dying format. Stick with satellite radio or online radio which gives everyone to ability to discover new artist and personalize their listening experience. Terrestrial radio almost programs people into thinking this is what is good music and what they should like and I believe that is wrong.

INTELLECTUAL PROPERTY

COPYRIGHT

In the U.S. once you create something of intellectual property it is automatically copyrighted. However, when you want to sue someone you need to register your work with the copyright office. We with the label release a lot of music so it isn't possible to copyright every song. It adds up in cost and time and isn't really necessary.

TRADEMARKS

I came up with the name "O-Town" as an artist name to release my hip hop instrumentals. I released three albums under that name. However in the summer 2017, the artist name "O-Town" was trademarked by the boy band O-Town. I had new issue with it and quickly released the instrumentals under another name I developed. They emailed iTunes and some other platforms to pull the releases down. If you feel like your artist name is going to be used forever, trademark it. Some artist change their alias over time but if your going to stick with it go ahead and trademark if you have the money and know how.

BUILDING A TEAM

When building your team either as an independent artist or independent record label you will need to find the right people.

At O-Town Records we have worked with employees, interns and contractors. We would get interns from the local universities and colleges and occasionally from out of town. But also have people who have just called asking for a job or internship when we didn't post any openings. They may have graduated a music related program or have worked in the industry and are looking for something better.

The bulk of our employees are artist managers or A & R. Our artist managers recruit new artist, develop them, produces, registers songs with the publishing and pretty much everything else. Our interns work unpaid, they sign an contract agreeing to this and an internship last from 8 weeks to 6 months. They help out with the artist managers. Each period they get a new assignment, a project to work on and complete.

Since most of our staff are working from a computer and phone, they can work from home. The industry standard is that artist managers work for a commission typically 10% - 20%. We have paid a small base salary in the past but this industry works off of results not time.

We rented a couple offices over the years. One on the east side of town and another in downtown. It was an executive office which could hold 2 desk comfortably and a board room for meetings. But was sort of unnecessary but helped in bringing together everyone under one roof. It helped from an image standpoint because some artist are skeptical of music business's in general so having an office helps with the image of being professional and established.

PUBLISHING

Register your record label with a performing arts organization such as ASCAP or BMI as a publishing company. We are registered as O-Town Music Publishing. SESAC is an invitation only organization. When you register your songs as a songwriter you are only getting up to 50% of those royalties. If there are multiple songwriters that 50% gets split up. Having the publishing company gives you the other half. The performing arts organizations collects royalties from many sources over a period of three months. Thirty days after that quarter is when a payment is sent to you.

The bulk of those royalties will be from streaming. Streaming only pays only a partial of a penny for every song played. So over time it add up to very little even with a lot of streams.

NEIGHBORING RIGHTS

Neighboring rights is a new way of collecting royalties. The publishing organizations do not actually collect all of the royalties for you and that's where neighboring rights comes in. Let's says you perform a show, you get royalties for the performance. Lets say that show was recorded on video and a DVD is put out. You collect royalties for that.

Let's say you do a performance one the TODAY show and it shown to millions of viewers. It can collect royalties for that.

LICENSING

Sync licensing is music licensed for the purpose of placing it in TV shows and movies or web media. A company can license the music directly from ASCAP or BMI then pays a lump sum and signs and agreement specifying the term. Or they may pay over time through a 3rd party licensing agency.

Another type of licensing is submitting through a 3rd party agency. They will place the music for example background music in retail stores and other uses not TV/movie related.

MECHANDISING

Many artist we sign come with their own merchandising such as shirts or branded sunglasses. We setup a commerce store on a sub domain which sells releases, O-Town branded shirts and other items. We then expanded to an actual fashion line on a new standalone website. We also sell on Amazon.

Merchandising is a great revenue stream and helps cross promote. We were approached early on by a merchandising company but decided not to go that route.

White labeling is taking a generic product and placing your logo or brand to the product. You can have the product fulfilled by another company or not. It's easier to have it fulfilled by a 3rd party company but they take a percentage of that.

SHOWS AND TOURS

Any artist today big or small will make the most of their income from live performance. Planning a tour takes months in advance. Use a website like indieonthemove.com to find venues and contact information. You can filter searches by city and state.

I recommend starting out dong a regional tour. Maybe two states like here we'll start with Florida and Georgia hitting all the major cities. If you live in smaller states probably a three state regional tour.

Once you start building and doing different regions you can eventually do an east coast tour or west coast tour. Eventually a nationwide and then international.

Make sure all the shows you are doing are paid shows. Some promotors and indie festival organizers will try a paid to play requirement for artist. Such scheme is that you pay the organizers directly for a spot in the show then you have to sell your own tickets to the festival. DO NOT DO THIS.

Must must be paid directly for everything you do. Try not to play to much in one area. This will over saturate the area. The more you play in one area the less people will come to see you. Unless it's a residency and the venue is paying you a flat rate rather then making your money from ticket sales.

Always negotiate with the venue a flat rate first. If that's not their policy go for getting a minimum and a percentage of either the bar or door sales. The venue should promote the show on their website and social media and you should do the same.

CONTRACTS

Written contracts are very important in the music industry. They protect the artist, the label and anyone involved. Anytime a producer is involved, manager or anyone becoming a part of your operation, a contract should be involved. We use 360 deals with artist we want to mainly promote and invest in. Our mega stars on our roster.

Our contracts are one year in length starting out with an optional two years to sign on by both parties. Doing that span of a year we start off recording one album. We release two singles, two music videos, promote it, do a photo shoot and do a regional tour. Each additional year we expand on this list so next time we do more singles, more videos and a bigger tour.

Make sure your main artist contract is looked over by an entertainment lawyer. During artist signings what we do is at first have the artist manager send over a proposal. The proposal will list all the services we will provide to the artist, the expectations of the artist, the deadlines and budgets. It is not a legal document at this point. Once they approve of the proposal we will send over the the actual multiple rights agreement or 360 deal. It's about 40 pages long and covers everything.

There is a clause for leaving band members if it is a group. There is also a section for arbitration so that disputes are settled out of court. We don't list specific budgets in the 360 it goes into a separate document.

When in talks of signing a new artist if they are well established at this point they mostly will have a manager. Send your communication through a company email, not a Gmail, or yahoo it looks unprofessional. You are dealing with industry folks at this point and it's best not make your record label or image look bad.

AFTERWORD

I hope that you find this book informative if either you are an independent artist, independent label or student. This book will continuously updated and additions added to it. It is by no means complete there is always updating and additional information to include.

About The Author

Lee is the musician and owner of O-Town Records, Inc.

www.leejonesbooks.wordpress.com

www.ingramcontent.com/pod-product-compliance
Lightning Source LLC
Chambersburg PA
CBHW030520220526
45464CB00006B/2877